WHEN I
LOOK AT PICTURES

WHEN I LOOK AT PICTURES

LAWRENCE FERLINGHETTI

PEREGRINE SMITH BOOKS

SALT LAKE CITY

This is a Peregrine Smith Book, published by
Gibbs Smith, Publisher, P.O Box 667, Layton, UT 84041

Printed and bound in Hong Kong by Everbest

93 92 91 90 5 4 3 2 1

Cover: *Dance Around the Golden Calf,* 1910, Emil Nolde.
Courtesy Neue Staatsgalerie, Munich

Design by Kathleen Timmerman

Library of Congress Cataloging-in-Publication Data
Ferlinghetti, Lawrence, 1919-
    When I look at pictures : poems / Lawrence Ferlinghetti
      p. cm.
    ISBN 0-87905-212-0
    1. Painting – Poetry. 2. Art – Poetry. I. Title.
PS3511.E557W46   1990
811'.54 – dc20   90-34070
                                                  CIP

For Nancy J. Peters

It must not wish to disarm anything; nor may the approved
triumph easily be honored —
that which is great because something else is small.
It comes to this: of whatever sort it is,
it must be "lit with piercing glances into the life of things";
it must acknowledge the spiritual forces which have made it.

Marianne Moore
from "When I Buy Pictures"

ACKNOWLEDGEMENTS

Paintings are from the following sources:

Cover: *Dance Around the Golden Calf,* 1910, Emil Nolde.
The Colossus, 1811, Goya. Scala/Art Resource, New York.
Promenade on the Beach, 1907, Joaquin Sorolla. Superstock, San Francisco.
Family of Saltimbanques, 1905, Pablo Picasso. National Gallery of Art,
  Chester Dale Collection.
The Equestrienne, 1931, Marc Chagall. Stedelijk Museum, Amsterdam.
The Kiss, 1907, Gustav Klimt. Osterreichische Galerie, Vienna.
Water Lilies I, 1905, Oscar Claude Monet. Museum of Fine Arts, Boston.
  Gift of Edward Jackson Holmes.
Place du Théâtre, 1898, Camille Pissarro. The Minneapolis Institute of Arts.
Appolo Sauroktonoa, 350-330 B.C., Praxiteles. The Vatican Museums.
Romantic Landscape, 1911, Wassily Kandinsky.
Bird Experiencing Light, 1969, Morris Graves. The Seattle Art Museum,
  Eugene Fuller Memorial Collection.
The Shrimp Girl, 1745, William Hogarth. The National Gallery, London.
The Finding of Don Juan by Haidee, 1878, Ford Madox Brown.
  National Gallery of Victoria, Melbourne.
The Morning, 1910, Umberto Boccioni. Superstock, San Francisco.
Tea, 1882, Berthe Morisot. Madelon Foundation, Liechtenstein.
The Luncheon of the Boating Party, 1881, Pierre Auguste Renoir.
  The Phillips Collection.
In Plato's Cave #1, 1972, Robert Motherwell. Courtesy of the artist.

Poems are from the following sources:

"Returning to Paris with Pissarro" is from *Lawrence Ferlinghetti: European Poems and Transitions.*
Copyright © 1988 by Lawrence Ferlinghetti. Reprinted by permission of New Directions Publishing
Corporation.

"In Goya's Greatest Scenes," "Sorolla's Women in Their Picture Hats," "Don't Let That Horse," "In
Hintertime Praxiteles," "The Wounded Wilderness of Morris Graves," and "One of Those Paintings
That Would Not Die" are from *Lawrence Ferlinghetti: A Coney Island of the Mind.* Copyright © 1958
by Lawrence Ferlinghetti. Reprinted by permission of New Directions Publishing Corporation.

"Short Story on a Painting by Gustav Klimt," "The 'Moving Waters' of Gustav Klimt," "Monet's Lilies
Shuddering," "Expressionist History of German Expressionism," and "Seeing a Woman as in a Painting
by Berthe Morisot" are from *Lawrence Ferlinghetti: Endless Life.* Copyright © 1977, 1978, 1979,
1981 by Lawrence Ferlinghetti. Reprinted by permission of New Directions Publishing Corporation.

"Oil on Canvas" and "The Painter's Dilemma" are from *Love in the Days of Rage,* published by
E.P. Dutton. Copyright © 1988 by Lawrence Ferlinghetti.

CONTENTS

IN GOYA'S GREATEST SCENES

In Goya's greatest scenes we seem to see

                                    the people of the world

       exactly at the moment when

          they first attained the title of

                      'suffering humanity'

        They writhe upon the page

                 in a veritable rage

                        of adversity

       Heaped up

              groaning with babies and bayonets

                      under cement skies

     in an abstract landscape of blasted trees

       bent statues bats wings and beaks

         slippery gibbets

      cadavers and carnivorous cocks

    and all the final hollering monsters

     of the

        'imagination of disaster'

  they are so bloody real

           it is as if they really still existed

And they do

    Only the landscape is changed

They still are ranged along the roads

    plagued by legionaires

        false windmills and demented roosters

They are the same people

          only further from home

   on freeways fifty lanes wide

      on a concrete continent

        spaced with bland billboards

     illustrating imbecile illusions of happiness

The Colossus, 1811, Goya. Museo Nacional del Prado, Madrid.

The scene shows fewer tumbrils
　　　　　but more strung-out citizens
　　　　　　　　　in painted cars
　　and they have strange license plates
　and engines
　　　　that devour America

SOROLLA'S WOMEN IN THEIR PICTURE HATS

Sorolla's women in their picture hats
stretched upon his canvas beaches
beguiled the Spanish
Impressionists

And were they fraudulent pictures
of the world
the way the light played on them
creating illusions
of love?

I cannot help but think
that their 'reality'
was almost as real as
my memory of today

when the last sun hung on the hills
and I heard the day falling
like the gulls that fell
almost to land

while the last picnickers lay
and loved in the blowing yellow broom
resisted and resisting
tearing themselves apart

again

again

until the last hot hung climax
which could at last no longer be resisted
made them moan

And night's trees stood up

Promenade on the Beach, 1907, Joaquin Sorolla. Sorolla Museum, Madrid.

PICASSO'S ACROBATS
EPITOMIZE THE WORLD

Picasso's acrobats epitomize the world

and there were eighty churches in Paris
                                which I
      had never entered
                      and my hotel's door
                                    smiled terribly
      and words were trombones
                    incoherent parrots
                    chattering idols

            but that night I dreamt of Picasso
            opening doors and closing exits
      opening doors and closing exits in the world

      I dreamt
                  he painted a Picasso in my room
            shouting all the time
                                Pas symbolique!
            C'est pas
                        symbolique!

Family of Saltimbanques, 1905, Pablo Picasso.
National Gallery of Art, Chester Dale Collection.

DON'T LET THAT HORSE

Don't let that horse
                     eat that violin

   cried Chagall's mother

                      But he
          kept right on
                  painting

And became famous

And kept on painting
                     The Horse With Violin In Mouth

And when he finally finished it
he jumped up upon the horse
                    and rode away
        waving the violin

And then with a low bow gave it
to the first naked nude he ran across

And there were no strings
                  attached

The Equestrienne, 1931, Marc Chagall. Stedelijk Museum, Amsterdam.

SHORT STORY ON A PAINTING OF GUSTAV KLIMT

They are kneeling upright on a flowered bed
  He
     has just caught her there
         and holds her still
   Her gown
      has slipped down
         off her shoulder
  He has an urgent hunger
      His dark head
        bends to hers
          hungrily
And the woman the woman
   turns her tangerine lips from his
     one hand like the head of a dead swan
     draped down over
         his heavy neck
     the fingers
      strangely crimped
       tightly together
  her other arm doubled up
      against her tight breast
  her hand a languid claw
       clutching his hand
  which would turn her mouth
        to his
  her long dress made
     of multicolored blossoms
     quilted on gold
  her Titian hair
     with blue stars in it

The Kiss, 1907, Gustav Klimt. Osterreichische Galerie, Vienna.

And his gold
        harlequin robe
                checkered with
                        dark squares
    Gold garlands
              stream down over
                    her bare calves &
                     tensed feet
Nearby there must be
        a jeweled tree
                with glass leaves aglitter
                  in the gold air
It must be
      morning
              in a faraway place somewhere
They
  are silent together
                as in a flowered field
      upon the summer couch
                which must be hers
  And he holds her still
               so passionately
     holds her head to his
              so gently so insistently
    to make her turn
              her lips to his
Her eyes are closed
        like folded petals
She
  will not open
         He
          is not the One

THE 'MOVING WATERS' OF GUSTAV KLIMT

Who are they then
                these women in this painting
              seen so deeply long ago
Models he slept with
        or lovers or others
               he came upon
     catching them as they were
              back then
       dreamt sleepers
           on moving waters
       eyes wide open
   purple hair streaming
          over alabaster bodies
     in lavender currents

Dark skein of hair blown back
           from a darkened face
      an arm flung out
            a mouth half open
       a hand
           cupping its own breast
  rapt dreamers
       or stoned realists
              drifting motionless
    lost sisters or
        women-in-love
       with themselves or others —
     pale bodies wrapt
          in the night of women
      lapt in light
         in ground swells of
               dreamt desire
             dreamt delight
  Still strangers to us
        yet not
          strangers
    in that first night
        in which we lose ourselves

  And know each other

MONET'S LILIES SHUDDERING

Monet never knew
         he was painting his 'Lilies' for
   a lady from the Chicago Art Institute
     who went to France and filmed
       today's lilies
         by the 'Bridge at Giverny'
            a leaf afloat among them
    the film of which now flickers
       at the entrance to his framed visions
        with a Debussy piano soundtrack
flooding with a new fluorescence (fleur-essence?)
   the rooms and rooms
       of waterlilies

Monet caught a Cloud in a Pond
         in 1903
     and got a first glimpse
        of its lilies
  and for twenty years returned
    again and again to paint them
      which now gives us the impression
       that he floated thru life on them
          and their reflections
    which he also didn't know
     we would have occasion
       to reflect upon

Anymore than he could know
    that John Cage would be playing a
      'Cello with Melody-driven Electronics'
        tonight at the University of Chicago
And making those Lilies shudder and shed
           black light

Water Lilies I, 1905, Oscar Claude Monet, Museum of Fine Arts, Boston.
Gift of Edward Jackson Holmes.

RETURNING TO PARIS WITH PISSARRO

I am in a painting by Camille Pissarro
Place du Théâtre Francais
Paris in the Rain 1898
only it is not 1898
It is 1948
a slight juggling of numbers
and no horse carriages
but the same eternal feeling
sad and elated
walking in Paris in the rain
I can feel it coming through
the French canvas
the light rain falling
out of the pearl skies
the Opera a deep pearl
in the far distance
of the Avenue de l'Opéra
And the domed roofs of the Théâtre Francais
the stricken winter trees
the smell of Gaulois at the Metro entrance
(which doesn't exist yet in the picture)
the fountain in front of the Théâtre
still spouting in the rain
And the dark chimneys
above the wet mansard roofs
above the fifth floor running balconies
and the grey awnings along the Avenue
dark figures under umbrellas
two by two
or clustered at corners
The grey Paris light
lies on the great buildings
like a light gauze veil
the lucent light
glimmers on the wet paving

Place du Théâtre, 1898, Camille Pissarro. The Minneapolis Institute of Arts.

on the sidewalks under the trees
You can almost hear
the clop-clop of horses
drawing the fiacres
The rain has let up
It seems about to clear
the veil to be torn away
pearl about to open
in the sky of 1948 –
I am *twenty*-eight
with new eyes alight
returning to Paris with Pissarro
from the New World

IN HINTERTIME PRAXITELES

In hintertime Praxiteles
                                   laid about him with a golden maul
striking into stone
                  his alabaster ideals
uttering all
        the sculptor's lexicon
                         in visible syllables
He cast bronze trees
                      petrified a chameleon on one
made stone doves
                fly
                  His calipers measured bridges
and lovers
                and certain other superhumans whom
he caught upon their dusty way
                  to death

They never reached it then

                      You still can almost see
their breath
                  Their stone eyes staring
thru three thousand years
                allay our fears of aging

although Praxiteles himself
                at twenty-eight lay dead

for sculpture isn't for
                young men
as Constantin Brancusi
                at a later hour
said

Appolo Sauroktonoa, 350-330 B.C. Praxiteles.
The Vatican Museums.

EXPRESSIONIST HISTORY OF GERMAN EXPRESSIONISM

The Blue Rider rode over The Bridge into the Bauhaus
on more than one blue horse
Franz Marc made his blue mark
on the blue scene
And Kirchner cantered through the dark circus
on a different dark horse
Emil Nolde never moldy danced boldly
around a golden calf
Max Pechstein fished in river landscapes
and fooled around with his models
(They all did that)
Rottluff painted his rusty lust
and Otto Mueller ate cruellers
as his painting got crueler
Erich Heckel heckled himself with madmen
and thereby foresaw their mad ends
Norwegian Munch let out a silent scream
Jawlensky made Matisse look mad and Russian
And Kandinsky grew insanely
incandescent
Kokoschka drew his own *sturm und drang*
Käthe Kollwitz chalked the face
of Death and the Mother
Schwitters twittered through trash cities
and Klee became a clay mobile
swaying to the strains of the Blue Angel
Otto Dix drew a dying warrior
on his steely palette
Grosz glimpsed the grossest
in the gathering storm
Max Beckmann saw the sinking of the Titanic
and Meidner painted the Apocalypse
Feininger traced a Tragic Being

Romantic Landscape, 1911, Wassily Kandinsky. Städtische Galerie im Lenbachhaus, Munich.

and fingered skyscrapers
which fell across the Atlantic
(and the Bauhaus in its final antic
fell on Chicago)
Meanwhile back in Berlin
Hitler was painting himself
into a corner
And his ovens were heating
as a Tin Drum began beating

THE WOUNDED WILDERNESS OF MORRIS GRAVES

The wounded wilderness of Morris Graves
   is not the same wild west
         the white man found
It is a land that Buddha came upon
        from a different direction
  It is a wild white nest
     in the true mad north
         of introspection
    where 'falcons of the inner eye'
        dive and die
     glimpsing in their dying fall
       all life's memory
        of existence
   and with grave chalk wing
       draw upon the leaded sky
  a thousand threaded images
      of flight

It is the night that is their 'native habitat'
  these 'spirit birds' with bled white wings
    these droves of plover
      bearded eagles
       blind birds singing
        in glass fields
  these moonmad swans and ecstatic ganders
          trapped egrets
      charcoal owls
        trotting turtle symbols
  these pink fish among mountains
       shrikes seeking to nest
    whitebone drones
      mating in air
   among hallucinary moons
  And a masked bird fishing
      in a golden stream
  and an ibis feeding
    'on its own breast'

Bird Experiencing Light, 1969, Morris Graves.
The Seattle Art Museum,
Eugene Fuller Memorial Collection.

        and a stray Connemara Pooka
                        (life size)

And then those blown mute birds
                    bearing fish and paper messages
        between two streams
                    which are the twin streams
                                    of oblivion
            wherein the imagination
                        turning upon itself
            with white electric vision
                        refinds itself still mad
                and unfed
                        among the hebrides

HORSES AT DAWN

The horses the horses the wild horses at dawn
as in a watercolor by Ben Shahn
they are alive in the high meadow
in the high country on the far mesa
you can see them galloping
you can see them snorting
you can hear their thunder distantly
you can hear the small thunder
of their small hooves
insistently
like wood hammers thrumming
on a distant drum
The sun roars &
throws their shadows
out of the night

HORSE IN AMSTERDAM, AFTER REMBRANDT

If I could read the blazed face

of this huge horse at night

with its hair like black flame

and its eyes charred chestnuts

I would want for words to tell

of the deeps drowned there

and the dumb world muted there

where the souls of dark trees

raise their raving arms

And nothing stops the stoned night

in the wilderness of its eyes

'ONE OF THOSE PAINTINGS THAT WOULD NOT DIE'

'One of those paintings that would not die'
    its warring image
        once conceived
    would not leave
       the leaded ground
  no matter how many times
       he hounded it
         into oblivion
Painting over it did no good
   It kept on coming through
       the wood and canvas
  and as it came it cried at him
       a terrible bedtime song
   wherein each bed a grave
        mined with unearthly alarmclocks
    hollered horribly
       for lovers and sleepers

THE FLOWER SELLER AT
COVENT GARDEN 1989

A great great great granddaughter
                    of Hogarth's Shrimp Girl
        the flower seller at Covent Garden
                    singing out in a voice
        straight out of Shakespeare

Fair and buxom
        skin like milk
                fishwife cap
                    and flowers in her hair
She tosses back her head
                        with piercing cries
        her sweet high voice singing out
                    like a songbird swooping
        over the madding crowd

The Shrimp Girl, 1745, William Hogarth. The National Gallery, London.

"DON JUAN DISCOVERED BY HAIDEE"

Hot dog I got me a naked lover
cried out Haidee
when she discovered Don Juan
lying knocked out & naked on a lonely strand
in Ford Madox Brown's old classic painting
and Don made it to the beach with an oar
even though his boat had a hole in it
and lay overturned on some rocks offshore
And here's Haidee hanging over Don
and stroking him (God what a hunk)
while another pulchritudinous virgin
hovers about with a
wish-I'd-seen-him-first look
And well anyway it's a
fine golden eve at the end of the world
with promise of a hot night with
a beached knight
if only Don when he waketh up
and sees Three's a crowd
can somehow get rid of this other
swooning enchantress which
ain't going to be too easy on
this here desert island with
the last boat sunk and
him the last man in sight
on sunset earth

The Finding of Don Juan by Haidee, 1878. Ford Madox Brown.
National Gallery of Victoria, Melbourne.

BOCCIONI'S MORNING AND TWILIGHT

Ah the so-bright future
   in Boccioni's "Morning"
     the so-fresh meadows quivering
         in the still early light
    the Naples Yellow sun
          very pale upon
     draught horses drawing wagons
          on wide rutted roads
   bright figures hurrying
       to newborn factories
a high church tower in the far distance
       full of rising sun
and a field full of light close up
   with yellowed grasses
    through which a woman in white
      with bundle under arm
        hurries toward some
         offstage affair
Ah but the Futurists were wrong
  in this so-bright picture of a future world
   bathed in industrial glory
      And Boccioni saw it too
        in his later "Twilight"
         of the same sweeping scene
in which the old day heaves a tired sigh
   as bent figures limp for home
     on dark roads narrowing
        to a red horizon
And dumb darkness descends
   upon a single stark figure waving farewell
    to the trembling future of the world

The Morning, 1910, Umberto Boccioni. Private Collection.

SEEING A WOMAN AS IN A PAINTING BY BERTHE MORISOT

Ah *tes cuisses*
as in an hour-glass
(through which all flesh flows)
at the cafe table now
you are living you are breathing
your bosom stirs
so slightly so lightly
belle plante bell jar
unaware of your self
full
of breath and life
not yet
awakened
I feel your breath so light
across the loud cafe
dear distant one
the time will come
or will not come
when we shall know
why we live and why we love
the time will come
or will not come
when you'll awake
from your deep dream of youth
the time will come or will not come
when we shall know
why all things pass
through the hour-glass
and why we now are here
in the late morning
listening to a juke-box Puccini
and looking away from each other
as if we did not know the music
as if we did not know the melody

Tea, 1882, Berthe Morisot.
Madelon Foundation, Liechtenstein.

LATE IMPRESSIONIST DREAM

In a late Impressionist dream I am riding in an open touring-
car with a group of French women in summer dresses and
picture hats with uncles in grey doeskin vests and striped
shirts with armbands and everyone is laughing and chattering
in French as if no other language had yet become socially
accepted And we get to an outdoor cafe by the Seine on the
outskirts of Paris as in a Manet painting under an arbor by
the river drinking wine and eating a grand picnic out of
wicker hampers And at the next table a group of French intel-
lectuals are indulging in their famous *grande logique* proving
that such-and-such is really an oxymoron And just then some
loud young men drift by in punts on the river looking sheep-
ishly like young American college students singing a drinking
song about Whiffenpoofs and we go on talking French as if
nothing else in the real world were happening anywhere And
all the people around me turn into characters out of Marcel
Proust and we are all in Swann's Way in a budding grove
with a straight Odette chez Swann but then of a sudden Blaise
Cendrars bursts in waving a newspaper headline screaming
"L'OR! L'OR!" and gold has been discovered in California
and I must leave immediately to join the Gold Rush and wake
up in my cabin in Big Sur looking like a French Canuck Jack
Kerouac and hearing the sound of the sea in which the fish
still speak Breton

The Luncheon of the Boating Party, 1881, Pierre Auguste Renoir.
The Phillips Collection.

OIL ON CANVAS

So once upon a time there was this little village called L'Huile-sur-Toile – a little tiny village on a little tiny river called the Toile. Now, that was a very long time ago, maybe in the Middle Ages or earlier still. Before that, painters mostly painted on wood – *huile-sur-bois* – but then, L'Huile-sur-Toile started growing, and more and more painters constructed *paysages* all around the banks of the Toile, and the little town grew larger and larger and larger, with all kinds of different neighborhoods or *quartiers* springing up, all built in different styles, and the styles swept the town from one end to the other, age upon age the styles changed, like the changes in architecture itself, like the changes in dress and in life-styles. There was the pastoral and then the Gothic *quartier* and then the baroque *quartier*, and eventually the symbolist and the surrealist and every kind of neighborhood that any artist could imagine. But at first there was mostly darkness on the Toile, because it was still the Dark Ages, and they only had candles and oil lamps and no electricity, and their heads were full of shadows and superstition and darkness too. But – but gradually the light grew in the heart of darkness, at first only a faint light in the distant sky, behind the dark landscape, behind the dark buildings along the Toile, and then it broke through over the rooftops, and flooded the Toile itself. Then the forces of darkness entrenched themselves on the Right Bank and the forces of light took the Left Bank as theirs, so that from the earliest times the reactionary Right faced the avant-garde progressive liberal Left, and each viewed the other suspiciously, each considering The Other Side to be treacherous territory, alien land. But the light kept growing, and then in the nineteenth century the first impressionists came marching down the boulevards from Montmartre to the river's edge, all of them looking obsessively for light and nothing but light, their easels under arm. And they strolled along the Toile and set up their easels and started painting the light, and some of them crossed over to the Left but many remained on the Right, where most of them had been born in good bourgeois families. But they all were obsessed with light and many of them didn't care where it came from or where it would lead them, they were not concerned with the sociology or the politics of L'Huile-sur-Toile. And their style swept the city and the suburbs and the countryside all up and down the Toile, as far as the eye could see in the new light, and swept even down to the far sea, through Normandy to Honfleur and back again, back past the Grande Jatte and the promenades and quays all along the Toile, and in the center of Paris-sur-Toile the good burghers of the city clapped their hands and danced and sang the "Marseillaise" and other stirring nationalist anthems, while the impressionists and the postimpressionists kept on painting everything in sight, including the Opéra and their own dear Bourse right here. And they painted Notre

Dame over and over, although neither the Right nor the Left could really claim the Church as being exclusively theirs, since it stood in the middle of the river on the Ile de la Cité, although many times the towers seemed to tilt to the Right and at rare times to the Left. There was one gang of artists who had descended from their Bateau Ivre high on the Right in Montmartre, and this gang refused to stick to the same style of painting with their newfound light but insisted on constantly changing their styles. Their leader was Picasso, who constantly broke up the old formulas and forged new styles of seeing and stole from everyone and invented cubism and painted everything all over in cubes and then destroyed them, after which came the dadaists and surrealists and symbolists and other ists and the taxis of the Marne and the First World War, while the painters all kept repainting the landscape of the Toile over and over, until finally the Spanish Civil War ushered in the Second World War, and with the Second War came the American invaders, and they came, they saw, they conquered but then didn't leave as they were supposed to, but stayed on to take advantage of the very good exchange on the American dollar and to take advantage of the very good light for painting. Then foreigners and others of their ilk from all over the world also started repainting the landscape of the Toile, only this time it was no longer recognizable as the adorable little *bourg* it had always been. It all began to look like a huge imitation abstract-expressionist canvas by Franz Kline or Willem de Kooning, while the Bourse went on looking just like it always had in impressionist pictures, with its inhabitants still looking and thinking like their impressionist portraits, and everyone rushed into the streets of L'Huile-sur-Toile waving the tricolor and shouting, "Don't change anything, ever! Don't rock the boat! The Left Bank doesn't exist!' And everyone went around acting as is the world of L'Huile-sur-Toile was perfect and no need to change anything ever, everything should go on as it always had on the avenues of La Grande République. But, but the students, *alors, merde,* the students — *ces enragés, ces chienlits* — were hungry and bored, and they had had enough of All That, they wanted an entirely 1new mix of colors, an entirely new palette, entirely new tools and new types of brushes to paint with, and they used spray paint on everything. They woke up the workers everywhere, they inspired the hunger strikers, and every other brand of forgotten humanity came pouring out of the side streets — the anarchists and the Trotskyists and the communists who hated everyone else, they all began to unite, because they were all hungry and fed up with the flat flabby *ancien régime* which didn't include them. They were all totally frustrated by the plutocracy that ruled the world even beyond the Toile, and they wanted to focus a huge magnifying glass on the canvas of the whole world and concentrate the new light on the very center of that canvas until it caught fire and burned a hole right through the whole landscape!

THE PAINTER'S DILEMMA

There they all were still, the unfinished canvasses, all chimeras, chiaroscuro illusions, dead stick figures still to be brought to real life, with their umbered pigments upon the canvas ground where formed the limbs the figures the faces of longing, yearning dogs and hungry horses' heads among them, the skulls with ears, liquid porches, spilling light, onto the canvas, pools of it forming into shape of eyes, but as soon as they were formed they ran down with too much turpentine and ran onto the dark dogs and horses, and they turned into echoes of laughter with every mocking sound a different color echoing about the canvas and transfiguring all its painted parts, horses' penises turned to yellow flutes that fitted to manifolds that fitted into female plumbing that in turn dissolved and floated down streets as yellow sunlight, while umbered shadows melted and percolated up into the gutters of tilted houses. Hunger and passion were what was needed but this got lost in the whirl of paint, in the depths of the cave that every canvas became, and the brush could not reach the boundaries of being inside Plato's Cave.

In Plato's Cave #1, 1972, Robert Motherwell. Collection of the artist.